Fictional books by the same author

Forsaken Knowledge
Lore of the Light Bearers
Stolen Fire
Robin Dead Hood and The Devil's Mile
A Funny thing happened on the way through the Cemetery
Galena-a short tale of the un-dead
My UFO experience-watch the sky
Flick

Non-fiction

The Kings of Sutton who?

Justine Norris book club on fb
Amazon author central

A note from the author

Let me explain that I am nobody of importance. I'm a single mum who has had to scrimp and scrape through life, and along the way I've learnt some harsh lessons, one of which is to take no ones word for it.

So although I can not compete in any way with proper authors, many of whom have writing backgrounds or at the very least have university degrees and can use the correct form of grammar, and make flowing sentences. (You will probably soon discover I don't know what a flowing sentence actually is) I do have the ability to see what other people don't always see, and more importantly, the balls to ask 'why'.

So judge not how I write, (I wrote like that on purpose) but what I am trying to convey.

Read with your heart as well as your mind and look beyond the wrongly placed apostrophes.

There are a lot of unusual words and spellings in this book, mainly to do with old texts, and if there are any errors, and I strongly suspect there will be, then it is simply down to my own incompetence, of which I hope you will forgive me.

Welcome to my world; a world full of questions, that many professionals can not answer, so I ask myself - if they know so much, why do they remain ignorant? And I don't mean that in a nasty way. Are we really lacking our own history that badly? And why are groups around the world, including Britain, still intent on destroying historical relics? Is there something in particular they wish to destroy, because of political or religious beliefs? It would certainly seem so. Of course this has happened on several occasions in the past. Books have always been burnt, from the sacking of the libraries of Alexander to the Nazi's in Berlin, and just last year there were attacks on museums, while the world sat back and watched this massacre from the comforts of our own living rooms. And so knowledge has been always been lost, but in this modern era shouldn't we be a little wiser and more tolerant than that, well apparently men still aren't.

Wow, that was heavy, but important, because when people burn or destroy manuscripts and relics then they make life harder for the ones that want to learn what's gone on in the past. Why this scares some people to death, I have no idea, but by their action they in fact automatically joined the 'ignorance gang.' I don't want to be in their gang, as I want to be smart.

I for one think that the past is interesting, and knowledge is something that we should not be destroying. Archaeologists can show and tell us how things used to be for people, geologists can tell us about the history of the earth, the historian can give us the cold hard facts and fictional writers can weave intricate stories out of thin air, like an magician waving a wand; forming life out of un-animated words and sentences, creating something beautiful out of some squiggles on a page, even if most of the time they've made the whole thing up. I think a good book would have all of these combinations entwined, don't you agree?

Silence is not always golden, especially when you want to know something.

So come along and journey with me on a discovery to find out who the Sutton Hoo man was, and let's briefly discuss if he could be King Arthur or a prototype for the saga of Beowulf, or whether it was the other way around.

Well, at is stage I could be talking complete rubbish, but let's find out together.

This book is a test. It is a test to see if I can shred some light, and find something out that no one has thought of before. It is NOT a test to prove any experts wrong, they're experts for a reason, and I have not got a superiority complex. It is a journey of self education, while sitting in the comfort of my armchair.

This book is dedicated to three men

The first is to Mr Page, who will probably never come across this book. He was my History teacher, in secondary school and installed my love of History, as did Michael Wood, the historian, who also brought history to life for me with his excellent books, and TV programmes.

   And to my dear friend John Harris, who is sadly no longer in this mortal realm and will now never know of this books existence. He would, however, have loved to know what I found out with regard to the Roman knights who wore black armour.

August 2015.

A quick note to the reader, I shall try to remember to say where I'm getting my details from, and accredited the correct people with it, and then you will know where to look.

Ok, so it's only fair that I start with a topic of which I know little, if anything about.
I am aware that most people setting out to write a book, take a well known topic, but remember this is a test, so however stupid this idea is, it is one I now feel compelled to carry on with. After all, I figure that the worst that can happen is that I end up looking like a complete fool. Fingers crossed for good luck that nothing bad does actually happen. Not that I'm superstitious. Well, only a little bit. Oh ok, I'm very superstitious, but I'm trying not to be.
    I now promise to stop rambling. However, my words will not be as sterile as some of the other non-fictional books I have read.
    So I've picked out something that many of you are familiar with, but one that most of us have never bothered to look into.
    And that's why I've chosen Sutton Hoo.
    I really would like to know if he could possibly be King Arthur or Beowulf.
    The reason behind this is a simple one. I watched a TV programme on the Sky history or possible Discovery channel yesterday, which showed a helmet, that was apparently uncovered on an archaeological dig, I presumed at Sutton Hoo as that's what the people on the programme at that point in the show were talking about. But they then showed a helmet that had a golden dragon on its crest and I immediately thought of Arthur Pendragon.

Now I've seen the iconic helmet of Sutton Hoo on many occasions, normally on the front covers of books or in museums and it never shows a golden dragon sticking up from the top of it. This helmet they showed was completely different. That piqued my interest and got me thinking.

Then this programme, which as it turns out, was all about dragon myths, started talking about Beowulf. He was killed by dragon poison, well that I did know. I'd had to study that saga at secondary school, back in the 1980's. My class had to learn a verse off by heart, and still to this day, if I choose, I can re tell it. Wow, a whole verse, what a memory I have, I say while scoffing.

I use the term re-tell because that's how older stories were told back then, they were spoken aloud, so the storyteller would breath life into his words, creating, he didn't read dull black letters from a page, like you are having to do now.

As I looked out of my living room window and at the sunlight which was reflecting off the wet pavement (it had finally stopped raining) I realised that we still tell stories like that, but normally only when we read to our younger children. We should do this more often, it is a skill that us Brits are loosing. We were the best story tellers in the world, and great Bards came from our shores. There are still Bards out there, normally in Wales-thank goodness for tradition.

I realised then that I really needed to find out more about the whole subject. What I knew about Sutton Hoo could have been written on the back of a postage stamp.

Then I thought that many people don't know how to do research now-a-days, and what better way then to let the reader travel along with me, and basically find out stuff together. And that's when I decided to write this non-fictional book; a very easy to read- non fiction book. After all, this book is aimed at the average person, who probably had a normal, and we live in Britain so probably a bad, education, and not for university students. I've never been inside a University, though I did have a couple of day trips to both Oxford and Cambridge once, does that count?

I'm sure there will be a lot of mistakes, a lot of dead ends and a lot of interesting things too, I live in hope. Half the fun is finding out things for your self.

So like a grave-digger, let's dig below the surface and see what lays there in the dark, waiting for us to find.

So let's start by asking a simple, if not slightly ludicrous question...

Sutton Hoo, King Arthur and Beowulf-are they one of the same person?

Well no, as Sutton Hoo is a place.
(I'm beginning to think that this could be the shortest book ever written).
Still I persevere, like Percival.
Have you ever noticed that the name and the word above sound very similar?
Well, its day one and I've come across my first stumbling block already.
Is it that the numerous stories of King Arthur are so complex that even proper scholars struggle with them- in my imagination I hear you ask?
No I reply.
So is it that Beowulf is so old and written in a foreign language, therefore you can't understand it?
No I reply.
As all the hard work of translating it for me has already been done by some clever person, and to get the gist of the original text is quite easy, just pick up a copy from any local book shop.
  So what is this major stumbling block? You finally ask, no doubt by now with a bit if irritation in your voice, or deep sarcasm, one of the two.
  Well, my laptop is old. It's missing a few keys and although apparently my internet is strong, it simply won't let me get onto it, so I can't do any research just yet; at least not from the comfort of my own sofa, which is one of the main points of this book. And at this point I will also inform you that I have no S key; so if you see a word with an S missing; now you know why. I'm being challenged in more ways than one!

Do you ever get the feeling that I'm not supposed to write this book? Or should I consider it a challange like the knight's of the round table and conquer any obstacles that come my way so that I can find the allusive grail?

Am I now being tested, in a modern 21st Century way? I ask myself, feeling slightly excited.

Well, lets' be realistic, probably not.., and my excitement drops down dead and dies a cold and lonely death. Oh, that was indeed a bad sentence, as my excitement has somehow managed to suffer a double death in only twelve words.

Well, I need some information somehow, so let's go old school.

To the local Library!

I am aware that as a sofa-historian I am kind of breaking my own rule, by walking out into the fresh air. Please forgive me all you couch-lovers, but it's hard to write notes down when you have no resources. And remember I haven't even visited Sutton Hoo.

At least the rain is holding off, after all, it is the heart of summer.

There were no books in the library dedicated to the topic.

So after coming back rather irritated, I made a quick cup of hot sweet tea and tried my internet again, and this time I could actually log on. I desperately need a new laptop, but they're expensive, and my job is a very low paid one, so, I must make do with this old thing.

Ok, so I have in fact just been on the internet. I personally prefer reading from books and using all available hands on resources, but this way I have to admit is a lot quicker, and I've already come across something that makes no sense.

I have already told you that I was watching a TV programme, but I am un-able to find the link to this. I've just tried again and I will keep trying. But the helmet they mentioned, and showed on TV, I think had nothing to do with Sutton Hoo.

Were they deliberately trying to deceive me, well no I don't think so. I think they were just trying to make the programme more dramatic then it actually was. I did like the CGI, but to be honest, I wasn't really paying that much attention to it in the first place.

After all, the only thing that had got my attention had been the dragon crested helmet, that I had just happened to see as I glanced up from the book that I was reading.

Oh ok, I admit TV was just on for background noise.

Going by my first quick look on the internet, the helmet, as I previously thought, has no golden dragon on it. According to the British Museum website, the Sutton Hoo one was covered with tinned copper alloy panels. It shows some pictures on it, not that they are clear to the likes of you and me, as they are in the Anglo-Saxon art-style, all swirls and strange beasts intertwining. One is of two men wearing horned head gear-again I thought that that was something not worn by the Anglo Saxons-so am I wrong about that too, because if that is the case, then a lot of TV programmes, and a lot of experts need to get their facts right.

Or are we talking shaman stuff here? The helmet also shows the depiction of a mounted warrior trampling a fallen enemy, who is stabbing the horse. There is also a hint that the experts think this might be some sort of spiritual helper, I wonder why they think that. If I was stuck under a horse and I had a sword, I too would be trying to kill it, especially if I was a warrior. I don't understand what that's all about. There is no one I can ask about that. **If you find out then please let me know. You can do this by going onto my website, which is http://justinenorris.yolasite.com**

You can check out this information for yourself by typing in 'British Museum-helmet from the ship burial at Sutton Hoo.'

It's apparently a late Roman Cavalry helmet from the early Anglo-Saxon period, dated to around the 7th Century from mound 1, Sutton Hoo, Suffolk in England.

So now I have two questions and only one answer. What was the helmet the documentary showed, and did the Anglo-Saxons wear helmets with horns? Apparently they did not, according to most modern experts. In my own opinion they would really interfere with your fighting. You'd always be poking your shield-wall mate in the eye. But at least I know that the helmet I remembered was the one that actually came from Sutton Hoo, the one without the golden dragon. I will now be chasing up this programme, because it is now bugging me.

So what I thought was going to be the easiest question to answer, has turned out to be nothing of the sort and has only raised more questions. Isn't that typical; any archaeologist will be nodding their head at that last sentence.

This is another reason why a lot of people don't bother to get self-educated, it's hard. It really is like a quest, and like Percival, you have to know the correct questions to ask, but unfortunately, we rarely do.

On with the quest!

So what do I remember about Arthur? Well, King Arthur, some say was a Duke, some say was a lout, and most people say he is a myth, was apparently on horse back a lot. So that means to you and me, he was in the cavalry, probably. He's normally depicted riding, and sometimes chasing the big old Celtic boar, on some mystical hunt, not to be confused with The Wild Hunt of both the Celtic and Nordic traditional myths. Now the Celtic side of things can get really complicated, and I'm not going to go into all of that, as that would end up becoming a book in itself. What I will say, is that if he did exist, then I would personally place him fighting the Saxons after the might of the Roman Legions had sailed away from Britain, and on their way to fight the Goths.

Why is that you should ask? Well because he would have been written about if he was real, and living before the Romans left. There are a lot of written records out there and I think it would be very unlikely that any Roman worth his salt and who had won so many battles would have let himself been left out of the Roman history books, had he been real and so very famous that his name has lasted for over a thousand years. Let's be logical about all of this. I mean we have letters written by mums to soldiers out on the Roman wall near Scotland, the Vindolander letters, asking if their son's need underwear and socks. You should read some of them because they're great; so if there had been some great hero at that time, someone would have said something. Or he would have been asking his mum to send over some pants from Rome, something like that.

But what if he was real?

There are books you can check out for facts, or as close as we can to get them. The most famous is The Anglo-Saxon Chronicles. I had a copy that had already been translated, but the problem there is, it's biased, and there are a lot of dates missing. I'm sure any expert could elaborate greatly on that, but I'm not an expert, and of course there is no mention about Arthur in them. There are many other chronicles. A lot seem to come from Wales. There are a few of the Irish invasion books/scrolls that are interesting, but I can't comment too much on them as I've never read them. (That is about to change). There are also the Welsh Red book of something or other, and a white book, and a black book. If you'd like to read or find out more, then go on your own quest and seek them out. Incidentally, I'm not that thick, I do know what they are called, but the fun is finding out for your self. Or if you can't be bothered to look them up, then just read on as I do cover some of their texts.

I'm going to leave some things unanswered in the hope that you look them up. (I want to write something sarcastic here, but I shall refrain, after all you are in fact reading my book, and I am grateful for that.)

So am I looking at AD 410+ to begin my search to find King Arthur? There are a few further clues, the place names of his battles, their supposed locations, but remember that even the experts can not agree on everything or even place where all of the battles took place, if they ever did. Many battle sites and places were named after the land, i.e. what the river at that location was called, or a tribal name. This was a big thing in Celtic and Anglo-Saxon times, as they re-named many places with who had taken them over, which only adds to the confusion.

Even people it seems, quite often have two names. Take for instant the Saints. St Mungo was also called Kentigern, apparently. That wasn't unusual. When the Romans took over Britain, many tribal leaders gave themselves a Roman name. It seems to have been a common practice.

My home town for instance could mean 'broken land'- which would not necessarily mean the land its self was broken, it could mean it was torn in two by fighting, or that there was a hill that divided the land, or it could later have been named after a man who owned it. Yes, it can all get very confusing, that's why the experts have such a hard time. Interpretation is also guess work sometimes.

But the main thing I have always wondered in connection with King Arthur was actually about pulling the sword out of the stone.

As far as I'm concerned that was an old Bronze Age way of making swords, using a stone mould, but that could possibly be confusing the whole concept, though there are writers out there that believe that he was a warrior in the Bronze Age. And this is not as far-fetched as you might think. The ancient Britons never wrote anything down, and we only have a hand full of stories that have been handed down to us to read. There are so many heroes that have been lost to time, so it's a really good point, and things have been forever lost to us. Boudica is a prime example, though we know she really existed because the Romans wrote about her. A few years ago no one had really heard of her or the awesome fight that she brought to the Romans, we'll, until her army failed. Now any British archaeologist would scoff if a college didn't know her name.

In ancient Egypt, names have been scoured out of stone, and their identities obliterated for one reason or another. I'm not going to go into that, it is not what this book is about. However, that too is really interesting, and something that will, if studied will open up a vast avenue of thought.

It is really difficult, because there are many theories out there, too many stories that had been worked and re-worked over the years and things have just got really complicated. If only they had the internet in the 5th Century. Then again, if you think of all the rubbish that is now circulating the web, I sometimes wish that it had never been invented.

Personally I couldn't care less if Arthur lived or if he was just a tale. My main concern is finding out the truth. Whatever than may be, which helps a lot when you are trying to solve a mystery. Be un-biased, and treat facts as facts and theories as what they are. Just because someone has a good theory it does not mean it is correct. You should treat this book in the same way.

So we have entered into the time of the Dark Ages. We have been told that they are called this because there is not much written information that has come out of this time, and therefore we are kept in the dark, well that's all well and good, but I have noticed that just recently we are beginning to glorify and modify history, and I think this is a major blunder.

In my opinion, the dark ages were dark. They were times of brutality, and if you don't agree then look up what happened to the monasteries and the monks in those times. Lindisfarne is a good place to start. It was attacked by the dragons from the sea, and by that I mean, Vikings.

They were times of death and fear, and yes some people did make some good jewellery but let's face it, if you've got an army of very scary-looking men intent on raping your daughters, stealing your animals and killing you, wouldn't you call them the dark days?

But I digress.

So at this point, I have to say, the Sutton Hoo warrior, chief or what ever he was is still in my book a good contender to be King Arthur, or Beowulf or at least to have been a man to inspire the first stories. Fighting a dragon could of course just be a way of saying fighting a man of the dragon, in other words a man who was a raider on a dragon ship and therefore a Viking. But they also really believed in the existence of physical dragons, so make up your own mind on that one.

So let's find out what the Sutton Hoo man's name was. After all, how difficult can that be? There must be some written record, perhaps on a grave stone?

There is no grave stone.

Well, once again it's not as easy as it looks. When Mound 1 was excavated in 1939 (according to the British Museum, which is what I was just reading on the internet) there was no actual body found. The soil was acidic apparently and had destroyed everything organic, well except leather from horses' bridles etc. There were no bones either. Was a man ever placed there I wonder? There were, however a few coins found in a beautiful purse (have a look on the Sutton Hoo or the British Museum websites, to view them) that were dated around 610 AD-635. There were Frankish gold tremisses, what ever they are.

So does that mean he was a Frank? Well that would tie in nicely with the French King Arthur story, the version written by Sir Thomas Malory, well at least one of them. But no, it simply means that if a body was ever there, he had a few coins placed into his grave with him. I expect he thought at some point he would find a pub in the after-life, and why not.

The most famous writer of King Arthur was of course Sir Thomas Malory with his book Le Morte D'Arthur, or the death of Arthur. I'm not going to go into that, it's easily available to buy, already translated and there for you to read, and I recommend that you do, it's fabulous. If you're skint, then look in your local charity shops and you'll find a copy at some point. I did on several occasions.

But getting back to Sutton Hoo, there are contenders of course for who was buried there. The main one of course is Raedwald, who died around 625 AD. It could also be his sons Eorpwald, Sigeberht or Ecgric. But no one really knows, so in truth it could be any one.

I've just checked the Anglo-Saxon Chronicle for that year, and there is no mention of Raedwald's death, but that doesn't actually mean much, as there are dates missing, and not everything was recorded. After all, it is just one source, and I'm very rusty when it comes to researching, I'll look again later.

All we know for sure it that he was highly thought of. Now we have to remember that a poor man could be given gifts from his Lord, and so we don't even really know the status of this man. Even King Arthur in some stories is portrayed growing up fairly poor, with Merlin looking after him, one boy and one man all alone in the woods-and I'm not going to share any more thoughts about that!

Let's look further into the ship burial. There was also Byzantine silverware, gold jewellery, a feasting set, and some textiles that had once adorned the walls, presumably of the ship, which only left an imprint in the earth. It had been 27 metres long. It was in the style of a long ship. Now what I find interesting in that list is the feasting set.

Normally the only people that would have that would be people of a high status that could afford to supply a feast to his men, so presumably a king, Lord, Bishop; people of that kind of wealth. So I'm going with the idea that he was a person of money and status, which would also mean that as from a young child he would have been schooled in the gentle art of swordplay. In other words he would have been trained to kill. He would have been groomed in the art of being the Boss, and he would be a hero, if he won battles and basically stuck up for his people and didn't let them get killed by whatever enemy he was facing. To others he would be an enemy, but presumably he fought for 'our' side which makes him a good guy.

In truth, I doubt there were many 'good guys' about at the time.

This man is still a contender for the idea of King Arthur, but does he have a sword? I mean, come on, he's a warrior so he should be buried with one.

It was a very good sword. Complex with a pattern that kind of resembled fish scales or a snake's wriggly imprint upon it, but that was only due to the technique of making it, again, I'm not going to go into that, if you had wanted to know how swords were made in Anglo-Saxon times, you would have chosen a different book to read.

It was gold hilted, the pommel was inlaid with garnets-red stones like rubies, only cheaper. I have a habit of loosing garnets, so that wouldn't have been my choice of colour of stones. They look gold against the gold though.

There were worn patches, suggesting that the sword was actually used, and not just for decoration for the burial. The scabbard was made of wood, bound in leather and lined with sheep's wool. I love that; because every time you hear the scraping noise the blade makes as it's pulled out of it scabbard, that grating sharp metallic noise they seem to love in films, then think again, what in sheep's wool? You also have to remember that swords were protected by magic; it wasn't just a symbol of power. They often had names and were thought of something much more than just a weapon; even the way they were forged by the smiths had magical implications; if you want to find out more about that then look up Wayland Smith and his seven swords.

There, you've discovered something else. In fact you have discovered two things, one, that the films are normally wrong, about pretty much everything, and two, this blade was used. This is important. Unfortunately it didn't have the name Excalibur etched into the lethal steel grey blade- why is life never that easy, but don't despair, because that particular sword was apparently thrown back into the lake anyway, where the lady living under the water, kindly re-caught it. Arthur in fact had two swords according to the stories. Look at the Celtic stories and Thomas Malory's book of King Arthur to read all about that, it's just after he's died, but not burned or buried, for according to the tales, he was taken to an 'island' by nine priestess'. Though, at some point he and his men were then buried in a hill and now await a time when Britain needs them. Was Sutton Hoo a burial mound? Well yes it was, obviously, but was it ever an Island?

Now this question may seem a little strange and slightly off the wall, but you have to remember that a lot of the marsh land in England, and the rest of the UK have over the years been drained. Before that, there were many more Islands in land. The most famous is Glastonbury. This place is also steeped high with myths and legends concerning King Arthur. So my question is not as far fetched as it may at first seem. Glastonbury is famous due to the monks finding King Arthurs grave, but if you read about that you'll notice the whole affair was terribly iffy, and again rather interesting, especially because of all the money that that location still makes. Some of the shops there are very expensive indeed, but then that's just carrying on where the monks left off. The Tor (the big hill) is steeped in tragedy though, and if visiting the place, maybe you should check it out, or say a prayer for the brothers. It involves hangings, a nasty King and the sack and destruction once again of knowledge.

Ok so what else?

A question I want to ask is, if Arthur was a cavalry man, is there any proof in the burial chambers at Sutton Hoo. Well, here we can open up a can of worms. Let's look at the Roman Catafrac quickly. They were a Roman Cavalry unit, who wore full battle armour, as did their horses and they really did resemble medieval knights, only they were around a thousand years before medieval times. Their amour was reputed to be so solid, that as far as I remember, they didn't use shields. No, I'm not making this up. This really could be a link to Sutton Hoo and King Arthur and I am sure there are many men looking into this as we read. Just type in catafrac and you'll get the whole story. I'm using the old spelling, and not the new one. The other important thing is that their helmets were VERY much like the ones found in Sutton Hoo, so am I right, can the Sutton Hoo man be what we think of as King Arthur, well, so far, yes he still can be. Woo Hoo and hazaar!

Except that the grave at Sutton Hoo that has a horse inside it, also has a shield.

Well, if you look up the National Trust-the royal burial, mound 17, there is a horse and a man in it. The man was about 24 years old, a little too young for King Arthur, but I've no idea how old the horse was. The man was buried with his weapons, and everyday items. I'm beginning to think that the whole site was dedicated to one man and his unit or family. I now need to find out if this is true or not.

Actually why is there a body in that grave, but not in the ship one? I'm not going to answer that, it's a question for the experts. Surly that ground too would be acidic?

Sutton Hoo is huge grave yard, but were there a large number of men buried around the same time. Because if there was, then that could indicated there had been a big battle, and all the fighting men were buried together-well the dead ones only, obviously.

Well, firstly, the whole site has not been excavated, so no one can possibly know at this point all of its secrets, but there is evidence in this case that strongly suggests I'm wrong. So let's find out what we can.

I looked up The Sutton Hoo Society, and they informed me that the cemetery was in use from the 8th-11th century, though they could just be referring to one bit, where there are post holes that indicated that there could have been a gallows at the eastern edge of the cemetery, but we have already been told by the British Museum that some burials were a lot earlier than that. So my conclusion is that it was a place of death for a very long period of time and that we are looking at a lot of different people being entombed there over many different generations.

The Dark Ages are proving to be difficult to tackle, and maybe the experts are correct, because I would like to know why no one thought to write down a name.

Going back thousands of years, we have graves that are marked. Look at some of the stunning Roman ones that are exhibited in Bath, at the Baths. And yet, here in Sutton Hoo, there is nothing. Are you also wondering why not?

So am I convinced that either Arthur or the Sutton Hoo guy was a Roman? Well, no I'm not actually. His helmet might have been in the cavalry style, but his sword was not. There are strange things happening in the graves, too strange to suggest he was in any way Roman, so I must be incorrect in saying that I think he was active straight after the Romans left, except that wasn't really what I said.

In the site at Sutton Hoo there really are some weird things happening. It has been said that there could be sacrifices there, which the experts know to be a very Viking way of doing things, and we know the site was used over a long period of time. There have been found, cauldrons, of bronze and silver, if I'm not mistaken, that are very Celtic in design, but their association with the dead is not clear. Although the Celtic Bran had a wonderful cauldron which brought dead warrior's back to life, and one of which I used in a previous book, Galena-a short tale of the un-dead.

Celtic mycology is something that is also hard to tackle, and a lot of people get very annoyed when you ask questions they can not answer, or you come across links that they have not seen, especially the numerous groups on social sites. They seem to hate it when your point of view differs from theirs. I used to belong to a few, and then I got annoyed at how people were treated by these so called self made experts. They are not experts; they are in fact very ignorant people trying to claim to understand something that they have tunnel vision in. Don't get me wrong, there are people out there that do know what they are talking about, but my recommendation is, to only get involved with an established society, to begin with, and learn from them, and then you can visit the public sites. That way you can tackle the know-it-alls, head on!

Rant and rave over. Thank you for bearing with me.

Maybe I should now give you a very easy timeline. In order; Celts, Romans, Anglo-Saxons, Christianity/monks and pagan beliefs running at the same time, later comes the likes of Harold, and the Franks, The Vikings and the Normans and there I shall stop as any thing further will not be covered in this book.

I've placed this simple timeline down because I think it might help, as they run in together quite often.

Getting back to Sutton Hoo, the Celtic cauldron could have been an heirloom, something he pinched or was simply given to him after death. They didn't go in for funeral flowers then, well actually they did, but again that's another story.

The Celtic hanging bowl (again see the British Museum for details) is beautiful.

It wasn't the only Celtic thing found. But then if you take a closer look there are a lot of Anglo-Saxon things too.

But none of this shreds any light as to who he was, because there was no name. So let's leave Sutton Hoo for a little while and have a look at something else.

Old Heroes

Beowulf is a very famous story. The facts you can retrieve easily from the www.

It is an old English poem, written around 700-1100AD- depending on which expert done the translating, the words used or the age of the manuscript he or she were working from, plus a lot more technical stuff (so roughly the same time as Sutton Hoo).

He is a Scandinavian warrior-hero who has epic fights with a monster called Grendel, and his mother. He then goes on to slay the monster of the deep, in great, glory, gory detail. He then becomes King and eventually when he starts to grow old he goes out once more to slay a dragon, which's become a bit of a nuisance. He manages to kill it but he is mortally wounded by its poison. He is then buried in a mound in Geatland.

The full poem survives in manuscript form, called the Nowell Codex, which is located in the British Library. The author is unknown, but is that such a bad thing?

Again, we have to take a step back in time and really appreciate the stories that were spoken round a roaring open fire, in the heart of winter, as that was a good time to tell a story, as the days were short, and the labour less, especially if you worked the land, and most people at that time did just that.

Beowulf was the normal type of tale that would have been circulating at that time. The world needed heroes, people that young men could aspire to be. The world was a dangerous place, the average person died in their 30's, and the hero dies a heroes' death, and does not grow old, or suffers a straw death-see the Vikings myths to find out more about that. Dying a hero is a reoccurring theme, and had probably been one long before Celtic times. The same could be said for a lot of religions, even in this day and age. Now that is something interesting to look into.

The same can also be said for King Arthur, for both are Kings who die a hero's death, in battle. But then, what King didn't at that time. Harold (the 1066 guy) is a good example, and his failure to win the battle at Hastings changed the course of history of Britain forever.

There has not been a British king or Queen on the British throne from the time of the tribes.

Many royals have in the past spent a lot of time and effort legitimising their right to rule a foreign country, and protecting their family bloodline- which is easy to do when you hold the country in you hands, and have an army at you disposal. The result is that they lied and still do, but hey ho, they were, and still are the strongest so no one took them on. It really was the survival of the fittest.

Getting back, there are other similarities, when dealing with stories. The most noticeable is that Arthur and Beowulf both fight mythical creatures. I'm not really that bothered which tale is the younger of the two stories, even if they were originally spoken orally, though with regard to King Arthur, the experts are still out as to the original story, and who wrote it or re-worked it. It's a bit like the tales of Robin Hood and is incredibly complicated and I'm not going to tackle that little kettle of fishes. It could well be that Sir Thomas Malory is the original creator of that epic tale, but I highly think not. There are many manuscripts that are a lot older than 'The Death of Arthur,' and that's not even bringing in the Templar connections, or the Christian and Pagan angles, or the really complicated Charlemagne, who has been proven to have definitely existed.

The main problem I now come across, it that it's hard to distinguish between fact and fiction. Just take a look at the many stories of Jesus. I'm using him only as an example, because a lot of people have heard of him. Some facts, some fiction, and he also fought demons.

Maybe we just have to remember that people love stories, and attribute stories with people that really lived and whom they loved.

What, don't you believe me, well ask any dedicated fisherman how big the fish was that he caught. I guarantee it was 'the biggest fish ever,' and that's just the tip of the ice burg.

There are some fascinating links with T. Malory's story and the country of Malta, with regard to the King Arthur tale (and with a strong Templar connection there of course) but if you really want to study them then you need to realise it will take some years.

When I write books, I sometimes put my friends in them, but they become characters, and this is a really important part.....so I'm going to repeat it, my friends become characters.... so do you think I'm the only person to write like that? Obviously I have their permission, but many years ago, writing books was a way to convey messages. Some were coded, some in plain site, and others were political, about real people at that time, while others were hiding things. Again, the history of books is complicated but fascinating. And something you would need a lifetime to study.

The political, social and religious aspects of the Dark Ages, seem to me to be as dodgy as a witches brew. There are facts and mysticism all woven together and the stew is thick and glutinous, and it doesn't sit well in the mouth. In fact it has great big chunky bits, and I don't know what they are.

It's really a pity that there is hardly anything written down. In fact that's so hard to believe, that I actually don't believe it. That is my own personal view. I believe that there are a lot more books out there in the big wide world, some must lay forgotten in musty boxes in the basements of museums or are in a private collection so that unfortunately the rest of us peasants will never even know of their existence, but men are greedy and selfish and nothing has changed over the years.

So might the Sutton Hoo man also be considered to be Beowulf? Well, no. In Beowulf it is clearly stated where he was buried. Now isn't that interesting. Even a made up character has been given a burial mound, yet the Sutton Hoo warriors are still unknown to us. Though there is no reason at this stage not to consider that we might just find out who is buried there in Sutton Hoo.

Which came first, Sutton Hoo man or the saga of Beowulf?

Arthur, King of Britain was also given a place to rest of sorts; Avalon, though no one knows where that is supposed to be. But at least it was named. There is a place in Burgundy called Avalon, but again, which came first? And most people think that he was British, going by the older Celtic books, if they are indeed older.

You see names were much more important then than they are now. Which again makes me wonder why no one knows who the Sutton Hoo men were; a name carried your family tree, it carried your birth place, or it could tell people your trade. We treat names very differently in this modern age, and they very rarely have any importance, but back in the 'heroes age' it was very different.

So do I still think that the Sutton Hoo warrior is King Arthur? Well, no one can definitely contradict me, but I think it is more to do with a man showing the characteristics of the hero. Who is to say, which came first, the story of Arthur or the king, the chicken in the egg so to speak. Maybe Arthur was real, maybe his stories are part true, part magical, and why not. It makes the story much more interesting.

I can not believe that Arthur wasn't part real at least.

So in the stories we have a hero-king with a name, and on the other side of the coin we have a real warrior without a name, which I find rather tragic.

The real story will eventually be handed down to us by people that know what they're dealing with, that have studied for years to understand everything there is to know, or by someone who finds a tatty old copy of history book in a box, hidden in someone's back shed.

Remember also that Museums and other places of protection also support the foundations for making the dead come back to life. For the weavers of fiction take on their findings and with their art of sword-play, sorry word play (only an S separates the two words-the pen is mightier than the sword) they give the dead life. The word smiths conjure up the past, and make to spell- a good play on words that, to spell correctly is to write the correct sequence of letters to make up the word you want, like a secret code, but to cast a spell, well that's an entirely different matter. The two go hand in hand, in many ways, you just have to think about it. And that is what you have to remember when dealing with the past. There, magic and facts go hand in hand.

We all know that magic doesn't really exist, right? Well, ok, explain a carbon footprint. Explain why it is that when you're alone you can feel that someone is watching you, but you know there's no one there. Explain why people sense things, and that others don't. Explain how electricity works up in the clouds. Science has explained a lot, but science and magic also went hand in hand. I think we are a bit clumsy in our modern way of thinking, and that we don't really understand what others in the past have thought of as magical, or scientific. I'm not even bringing superstition into the conversation.

So where do I go from here. I'm going to have to tackle some of the Arthurs' stories for clues. Erg, wish me luck.

The tales of King Arthur, King of Britain

We have several sources that we can instantly go to. There are thousands of books written through the ages and I'm not going to talk about anything modern. That is because it is a hot topic and there are many people out there only too willing to slander and contradict anyone who dares to disagree with what they believe. It is like a religion to some people and to others it is much more.

Most people seen to concentrate on who he could be, and I suppose that you could come to the same conclusion with me, but remember, I'm writing this with a smile on my face, and I don't care who he was, it would just nice to know the truth.

I am going to keep to the well known stories; the one's you may already be familiar with.

Remember, this book wants to answer only a couple of questions, and it's not about proving anything. Unlike others, I don't feel the need to.

I have looked up a brilliant website, so go on the www and put in Mabinogion.info and it'll bring you to a site that is both pretty to look at and knowledgably. This site is clearly written and is very good for anyone wanting to understand the basics, without too much theory, dates and all that other stuff no one but the most studious is really interested in.

I have also logged this link onto my fb book club website, which is open to the public, and which you are welcome to join. There are rules, basically, just have respect for people using the club. I will take down anything or anyone who is not nice. Just look up Justine Norris Book Club.

The Mabinogi, pronounced Mabin-Ogion, was written in Middle Welsh and includes tales such as Culhwch and Olwen, as well as Arthur. He is a lot different in these versions. The book isn't really a book, more like a collection of tales, a bit like how the modern Bible has been made into a book from various writings. They again will give you an insight into the past, and they are beautifully written. Thought to be written in around the 12thCentury, 1350-1410, actually I might have got that completely wrong, as those dates seem way off, but apparently there are numerous dates ascribed to them and again it can get complicated. Especially when you think that the main people in the Dark Ages that were writing were clerics, scribes, monks. I always thought the stories were older than that. And then I remembered that they had been copied, a lot of things were, so the experts have to go with carbon dating and the style of writing to establish any date. I'm presuming they have the same problem with Beowulf.

But that isn't the best news. I've just stuck on the TV and the Nat' Geo channel have just started a programme dedicated and simply called King Arthur, viewed at 1 o'clock in the afternoon, on the 23rd of August, 2015. We shall be coming back to that later. See all you have to do is ask! And I've just noticed that an animated film about the boy Arthur and Merlin is also on later...stranger and stranger, must be Wyrd working again.

Welcome to my world. Anyone who knows me personally or has read my first three books will know that my life is sometimes a strange one.

Myths and facts woven into one!

So let's go back to the basics. The Welsh Monk called Nennius in around 830AD wrote in his Historia Brittonum (I'm now using my memory so I really hope I've got that right) that Arthur was a warrior and not a king. He fights twelve battles including Mount Badon and one near or at The City of the Legions. There are people out there that have their own theories as to where these sites were. There are a couple of good ideas and some really stupid ones too.

Geoffrey of Monmouth also wrote about Arthur, in around 1136. He has been slandered by some experts that see him as being fanciful, and there seems to be evidence to back that claim up, but it's a long story, and it is possible that he was copying from earlier texts, and weaving magic and myths, but they are still really good to. Just take them as they are and enjoy them. Maybe the experts are just jealous, after all, he had in his possession books and scrolls that are now no where to be found. He has imagination, and yes the facts are a bit iffy, but just enjoy his works. They are still valuable.

These old manuscripts are already translated for you, by very clever people who have studied probably for years, so take your time and acknowledge their dedication and skill, and the texts will give you a taste of the past. I for one am glad that Geoffrey wrote what he did. He also puts the death place of Arthur's father, Uther firmly in St Albans, and I really have to dig out the book that tells me that. That info, for me, was taken from a local book all about Hertfordshire and can be found in the local libraries. I've just gone upstairs to find it so I can jot the title and details down for you only to discover that it is another one that I've got rid of, only to need it later. The story of my life, I say with a sigh.

William Caxton published Le Morte D'Arthur in 1485, written by Sir Thomas Malory, but these stories are my least favourite. I prefer the older tales, and not all the lovey-dovey stuff and that infernal grail story. It's all too unbelievable and not something the real Arthur would have had time for in his day and age. And to me, it's all about rich people's vanities, and the idea of courtly love.

I dislike the grail story so much. There are so many people now looking for it, both physically and spiritually, and they are all drawing a blank. It's a book version of the philosophers' stone. There is so much involved with this particular story, that any one seeking it will in no doubt be driven mad just trying to find the damned thing. That's my personal view, don't retaliate. I have already stated I am no expert. I am also very aware of my choice of word; damned, which I use for a good reason.

Malory also, as far as I remember, gave Arthur the sisters Morgawse and Morgan Le Fey. They married King Lot of Orkney and King Urien of Gorre. His name will crop up again, later. Le fey is an interesting name, fey as in fey folk, and its links to fairy folk? Is this what Shakespeare latched onto when he wrote A Midsummer nights dream? Do you remember I told you that I think Malory played up to his peers and wrote them into his books like I do with my friends well so did Shakespeare. Not necessarily his friends, but he was most certainly was familiar with the politics of the day, and wrote what he considered would do well for him. I seem to be the opposite, for whatever I do, no one's still ever heard of my books. I know it takes time, but come on! Anyway Queen Elizabeth the first watched a lot of Shakespeare's plays apparently, so draw from that what you will.

Once again, I think that Malory was using his wily skill for the court at the time, bringing in rich people into his story and playing to their vanities, like I've just stated. That idea could be book in its self.

Merlin, sometimes called Myrddin Emrys can confuse things. It started with Geoffrey of Monmouth, again. But then when you realise that Merlin was a priest, possibly a Druid then you can hardly blame Geoffrey, for latching onto that type of thing, and no one knows where he got his information from.

33

You could just type in King Arthur on the World Wide Web, and see what you get. I'm telling you now you will be spoilt for choice,

So now let us go back to the National Geo TV programme and see what they have to say on the matter. Having not yet watched it, I can bet they'll be interested on trying to prove who he was. We shall see.

Ok so that was interesting, and a now I have a headache, major mind over load. Not because of the TV programme, but because of the research I've just done.

The programme was mostly concerned with the 'for and against' contenders for the real King Arthur, as I suspected that it would be, and was quite frankly a complete waste of time in that aspect, but it gave me some leads.

Before I go any further I shall tell you some of the links that I have just looked up.

The first www was kingarthursknights.com/faq/swordstone. And .fectio.org.uk.articles/draco.htm

And .marres.education/sarmatic_traces.htm   all of these sites are riddled with interesting information. You could also look up The Gododdin, which is very interesting also, and has links to what I just found out.

Which as it happens was quite a bit, none of which has anything to do with Sutton Hoo, but a lot that answers questions that I was asked by a dear friend last year, who is now sadly no longer with us on this earthly plain.

Typical, now I know the answer!

So forgive me while I deviate a little, but it still has some bearing on what I'm seeking.

Last year we were talking in his back garden. There was me, Noj and his wife, Chic. (I have her permission to include her in this book). Noj asked me who the Roman cavalry could be that fought with King Arthur.

He had been watching a movie, where the knights kind of wore black armour. He asked me if I knew if any Roman's had ever worn black armour. Well I didn't think that any had, so we had a bit of a chat about the whole idea of the Roman Catafrac (Roman knights in full battle armour) not that we knew about them at the time, and the film, but it's not a film that a lot of people like when considering facts about King Arthur, though the Merlin angle was interesting.

He also asked if I had picked up on the sign that the 'church man' had given Arthur on his forehead, (I think in the film they called him by the Roman version of the name, but I can't remember properly). It was a cross, but yes I had immediately realised that it was the mark of Mithras, rather than the traditional Christian one that you would expect actors to use in a film. That one tiny detail for me made the film ok in my book. Others have trashed it, but remember a film is a film and nothing more. I never fail to understand why people take things so seriously, when they are for entertainment purposes only.

Is this book going to be looked at by my superior peers and slandered because my thesis is not what they like? I doubt it very much. In fact because this book is not being circulated or marketed I doubt that it will even be looked at by anyone except me and maybe a few friends.

It is also my first work of non- fiction, and my name is not well known.

Anyway, so now that Noj is no longer around, I had inadvertently been given the answer to his question that I had failed then to answer.

Yet again I see the similarities between rne and Percival. I would have loved now to be able to pop round to their house and talk to them, as Noj would have loved to know what I have found out.

Instead I immediately phoned up Chic and told her about what I had discovered. She agreed that Noj would have loved to have had this conversation. And on a personal note, that is what I will miss more than anything, the three of us discussing subjects like this over coffee and cigarettes while watching the sun getting lower and lower in the sky.

This is also why this book is dedicated to him, it seemed fitting.

So onto what I found out. This took a lot of delving and it was hard work. But that is what you have to do to get answers to mysteries, but remember not to get lost yourself. One can easily become obsessed, that's why I choose humour as a safe guard.

You have been given the websites so that you can check them out for yourself.

The programme talked about the so-may-tion cavalry, it turns out that it's actually the sarmation cavalry. That's the problem when the programme doesn't put up the names. So that was the first obstacle, which took about ten minutes until I reached a site that linked up with the proper spelling.

My notes; The sword in the stone, claiming the right to be king was apparently one of their rituals and yes the mould thing I have previously said were rituals too. So was the lady of the lake-which could link to the old custom of the Celts where by they broke a sword and threw it into the lake upon a death, and possibly had connections to a water ritual that the Sarmation apparently performed. Well, that was no surprise.

Their banner was a dragon!

That is a connection.

Awesome!

I had made a few more notes but they were more related as to whom Arthur could be, and I am not really concerned with other people ideas, however intriguing they are.

So I typed, looking up Roman helmet with a dragon's head on them, which didn't help what so ever. All I got was modern day merchants selling their wares.

I was still on the look out for that helmet I had previously seen with regard to the dragon programme, this still alluded me.

I was then put onto a text called the Narts Saga. I had never heard of this, in fact I wasn't sure that this was a real thing, but apparently it is. And as it happens it's very interesting.

So back in 175AD there was a treaty between the Romans and the Sarmation, and the outcome was that they sent 8000 men over to the Romans to help out. So 5,500 formed into the 6th Legion Victrix and they were sent to Britain. Some were sent near to Hadrian's Wall one company the Ala prima samatorum, stayed at Bremetenacum, or Veteranorum or Ribchester (Lancs). This was happening in the 4th Century apparently. It is a little bit confusing, but I suspect fairly sound. They obviously didn't all leave the country when their term of service finished, and were given land in Britain. There was also the mention of grave stones proving all of this.

This was all very interesting, if like me you actually like history, but what has this to do with Arthur, well, there is also a story, where the hero in the ossetion tale lives on or in King Arthur. It has interlaced links with the Nart Cycles and has links to the Roman praefect Lucius Artorius Castus. I could have spelt that name wrong.

I will point out that I do get things wrong, so please check if you want to make a proper study of this.

The legend of King Arthur is first named Gwarddur in the poem entitled the Gododdin, and again this is really interesting. It is about a South Scottish clan which were defeated by Saxons in around 600AD at the battle of Catreath. Please check this as I don't always believe everything I read and neither should you.

So, by watching that programme I was able to find out a lot about the Knights, which like I've said was a question that was put to me, of which at the time I had no answer to; not properly.

I was led to some important and unknown texts, which is always good, and I now know what the Nart manuscript consists off.

Well this is all very good, but does it come anywhere to helping me out? In fact after reading all that lot, I'm actually trying to remember what my original question was; mind over load.

So let's leave the realms of knights with dragon banners firmly on these pages and lets turn to one of my favourite characters, that of Merlin.

Merlin

This is my favourite character for many reasons. Again there are various people that think that he was a lot of very different things; ranging from a mad man who couldn't accept that his friend had died and became a mad hermit running around in the woods in Caledonia, to magical wizard who could control the elements. To silly old man that got trapped by a much younger woman after having all of his secrets revealed and stolen.

Personally I prefer the traditional idea of him being a Druid. But there is a problem with this. The Druids as we have come to see them had already been pretty much decimated by the Romans when they attacked Mona, or to you and me, Anglesey in North Wales, at about the same time that Boudica (one of the spellings) was around. About 69 AD, and obviously that all happened a long time before Merlin was born. But we are now looking at the time of Taliesin, the bard, the Christian, the Druid, or what ever he was; influential maybe.

And talking of writing, there is a huge amount of confusion with Merlin's name alone, because it had been changed. In one language, French I think, though this could be wrong, it got changed because it sounded like a word that meant faeces. So although that could be rather amusing, it is not very helpful. There are people that think it meant 'Hawk', that's the easy version, or even 'tower', but let's face it, if you look long enough you can find connections everywhere, so I'm not going to dwell on his name or its meaning.

It is true that there could have been a few left over Druids so to speak, in the 6th Century. Well, the knowledge would have taken a fair while to die a slow and painful death and some 'priestly types' would have converted to the church, possibly the Celtic one for many different reasons which I shall not go into.

However, I can at this point introduce you to Taliesin properly. He was a bard at one point at the court of Urien, and this is where things can get interesting. There are names that just keep cropping up with regard to Arthur and Merlin and Urien is one of them. So we have Taliesin, who was very famous, and has a lot of writings and poems attributed to him, working as a bard in various courts. He is also mentioned in the Y Gododdin, and he was later glorified in the 12th Century, when once again we see a rise of Arthur in the romance novels in the French courts. The tales of Merlin by this time have been altered, and have become much more Christianized, as to be expected, but was Taliesin a Christian....hardly. I personally think that he had a lot of different influences, including Druid. Yes most of them had been wiped out by the Roman, but how many are we actually talking about. We know that some fled to France, Brittany, little Britain, we know that some went over the water to Ireland, and others to Scotland, so why would the records of Druids vanish completely. I strongly suspect they didn't, I think they were amalgamated with all the other religions at the time that swept the un-united Kingdoms.

I have a poem of Taliesin's, and he is writing about Mithras, and that I am convinced about. It is a beautiful poem. Rudyard Kipling wrote about both Taliesin and Mithras, he too is a glorious writer.

Now Romans had been gone from Britain for generations by the time Taliesin was born, in the 6th Century, officially, but of course that isn't really true, not everyone left with the Legions. Many prominent families still evoked Roman values, some were still running the country and some had by now just become a Christian land and wore different armour, or priestly robes, so it's not to far-fetched to realise that Bards would have been tapping into a myriad of sources. Well, remember, beliefs get handed down, it's that simple.

Incidentally, Taliesin wrote in Welsh, as many good Bards do. For Wales is the home to the Bards. It never was exclusive, but with the South East being taken over, the tribes there had already lost their identity because of the Romans and then they had to take on the Anglo-Saxons as well, and probably not through choice. Angle land became England. But that's another story. Wales by comparison had not lost its roots, unlike a lot of other parts of Britain.

But I'm getting side tracked, always be aware that that is something that is really easy to do. We really need to find these people.

In fact I would probably guess that just as many people who want to find Arthur, want to find the real Merlin too. Maybe not so many scholars, but a lot of pagans do, for obvious reasons.

He has been given the ability to shape shift, normally into a white heart, a white stag. The white heart is also the emblem for Hertfordshire, which probably has nothing to do with what this book is about, but it is an interesting fact. The white stag has very pagan roots, and is something that I have written about in the past.

The white heart was a beast that came from the otherworld. This is why it is pale in colour, white being associated with death etc... Being white also signifies purity and innocence, but that could hardly apply to a character like Merlin, who is often depicted as sly, like a fox. The white heart or stag also has connections to Cernunnos, the spirit of the greenwood and forests, and he is shown, often in cauldron, like the ones in Sutton Hoo, with antlers on his head, while sitting in a shamanic posture. (Back straight and legs crossed). The white stag is a questing beast, and is also in some of the King Arthur stories, I think? Yeah, he was always trying to catch it, that and the big boar; the Twrch Trwyth.

It takes time for customs to die, but if you look at The Morris men we have now, they remember the dances, but not necessarily why they were performed. There are still some remains that we cling onto and quite frankly we need to cling onto them because our traditions are in decline once again and now they risk being lost forever. Have you ever heard of Mummers plays? Like I said, we as a nation are loosing our identity. Our personal history has never been at such a risk as it is NOW.

My first ever book was called Forsaken Knowledge for a reason, but maybe I should have given it the title of Forgotten knowledge.

There are many attributes given to Druids. Shape shifting is one of them. When Uther Pendragon wishes to have sexual intercourse with Igraine, the wife of Gorlois, not that she had any say in the matter, Merlin changes Uther into the form of Gorlois. A despicable act if I ever I heard one. So taking on the form of her husband, Uther has his way. This act of shape-shifting is only to be considered as magical, what else could it possibly be?

This magical infused rape supposedly took place at Tintagle castle. Archaeologists have discovered that the site was possibly a Royal residence. There are foundation stones that are older than the medieval castle that people visit today. But did it ever belong to Gorlois? It would also make Arthur Cornish, as Uther would have taken both the woman and the dead kings Kingdom. We have Geoffrey of Monmouth to thank for placing Arthurs birth at Tintagel.

Talking of Cornwall, where is the wall, and does it have anything to do with corn? A silly question maybe, but lets' find out. Well, it was named after tribes of Britain, the Cornovii, to give you the easy answer, and there wasn't a wall but there was a big hedge. That's the shortened version.

Another thought, just before I forget, concerning the round table. The concept that all men were equal was not a new one, no matter what the experts say. The cult of Mithras had already taught that. There is a Roman connection to Arthur, and like the stories, all the religions were also mashed up, so beliefs would be too. Many scholars can contest this statement, but it is true. That idea has to be in the later versions, for men were not equal, they never have been and never will be, but it was a good fancy notion for the later French courtly ideals.

Those days you would see and be aware of many different beliefs and rituals, as to be expected.

In Geoffrey's Historia Regnum Britanniae, 1136 we find that Merlin has got a bit mixed up with Myrddin Wyllt (Merlininus Caledonensis) and I've no idea who with. Oh hang on, that was Aurelius Ambrosius if my memory serves me correctly. It was a very popular book, you have to try and remember that. Not by our standards, obviously. Merlin was a Cambion, that's to say his mother was a human but his dad was an incubus. His mum's name was reputed to be called Adham, which either sounds like Adam or a place name to me, but look at the prose, Brut, if you want to know more. Also Merlin was supposed to be imprisoned by the Lady of the lake, and that is very interesting. There is a story where he is trapped under a fountain, in France, but again, I think this is another version of the later tales. Or is it just all to do with the ladies at the court entrapping men?

Check out the web and look up sacred_text.com for more details.

Geoffrey's third book the Vita Merlini text was based on the 6th century version of Merlin (Taliesin times) the one that sees his brothers and friends killed, and where he ends up in the forest mad as a march hare. In this text however Merlin is a King and prophet of South Wales. The story is a bit depressing, but fascinating.

Ok, I apologise in advance, the next bit might be difficult for some people to follow. I have made it as easy as I can, but it's a mouthful to say the least.

This is the battle of Arfderydd, in 573. There are no references in the Anglo-Saxon Chronicle for this battle, or even this year, there may well be a good reason for that. It's got nothing to do with the Saxons, so why would they write it down? This battle as far as I can tell was Briton fighting Briton.

You could try cross referencing it with the British Chronicles. The battle is between Rhydderch Hael and Gwenddoleu. If you type in 'the year 573' this is what Wikipedia comes up with, give or take.

The battle of Arfderydd is fought between Gwenddoleu ap Ceidio and the sons of Eliffer, Gwrgi and Peredur or King Riderch Hael of Strathclyde. Though there seems to be a lot of others involved too. The forces of Gwenddoleu are killed and Myrddin Wyllt (possibly Merlin) goes mad watching their defeat-according to the annals cambriae. Once again, another name keeps cropping up, Peredur but it is Bedevere, who throws the sword back into the water, in the stories, but does he do this at this battle, and was he even there? Well, according to legend, and Wikipedia, he was one handed, and a bit of a lout, so if he was one handed, would he be fighting? I wouldn't have thought so. And yet he is classed as one of the knights of the round table. That makes no sense to me. He has also been given the role of dark magician, which could

44

tie into Merlin; both are thought to have used dark magic. Are we back to the churches way of thinking; that every druid is dark and evil?

Is Merlin real? Was he a King, but also a druid? If so, where are Arthur and Bedevere in all this? Was he too killed in this battle, or another? Badon was given as his last battle. Is that why Merlin went mad? Or is Arthur fighting in a different part of the land?

Now that could be a big key that will unlock a lot of unyielding doors, but I'm no expert, and that key is for the people that have been trying to figure this lot out for years. I wish them the very best of luck. It is almost madness to enter into the world of Arthur and Merlin, and I'm sure that many men in the past have had to suffer their own private madness trying to get to the bottom of the well of our minds. Let's hope at some point the lady guarding it will finally give up all of her secrets.

I could give you the names of the knights, but that will just confuse you, as their names have also been changed over the years, and again I am straying from the main topic of this book. Yep, tracing these people is difficult. I must remember to ask the Fisher King the correct questions. Otherwise I run the risk of being trapped in a labyrinth of knowledge, but going round and round the corridors of my mind forever, and ever lost.

I'm beginning to wonder if Sir Thomas Malory read these early battle texts and thought, 'blow this, this stuff is just too confusing, I'm going to write something that everyone can actually understand.'

I suddenly feel like I like him a lot better.

Another early text is held in the National Library of Wales and is called The Black Book of Carmarthen. So putting the ghostly images aside, (stick that into your search engine and check that out) we see that it was written in Welsh, probably by a monk, as it has links to the church. It is interesting because it mentions the battle of Llongborth, and Arthur too is mentioned. So could Merlin and Arthur both have been warrior chiefs? Was Arthur an under-lord?

And I feel like I'm going to blow your mind if I start recounting those text, umm, I'm debating, well really they need to be added if you want to try and prove that he existed. I'll give you a very short version.

One poem has Arthur and Cai confronted by a gatekeeper, but then the lord of the underworld Gwyn ap Nudd makes an appearance and it all gets a bit weird. There is also a poem that has burning books in it, which is what I have also talked about in the first chapter. And I'm going to leave it there.

Before I go further you can also check out Yr Afallennau text and Yr Oianau, which also show the mad Merlin, now smitten with grief, like a father that had just lost his favourite foster-son in battle.

If I had to place bets, then I would say that he was a real person and this is where you should start to look for them both. But remember I'm not an expert. I'm simply a woman looking for answers.

I still prefer the films characters of Merlin, the Druid but if I'm honest if he was real, then I suspect that he was a king. There has, after all, always been a link to Kings and magic, and sacrifice. Just look at the customs that are still performed to this day and then challange me!

Again, in the old days, a King was more than just a brutal man wielding a sword. There are many sacrifice connections regarding kings and queens, especially when you look towards the Celts, and their old customs and where better to start looking then in Wales.

But Arthur was from Cornwall.

The land's boundaries are so different now then when they were in the past. The land has changed and its owners have changed too. This is something else that you have to understand if you are going to start studying the past. I was once told that part of Cornwall was held by the Welsh at some point. Could this be true, well I'm going to leave that up for you to find out, if you're really interested.

Sometimes just typing in the most simple of questions rewards you.

You don't need to know all of the old texts, just simply ask a question.

Now let's turn to Scotland, which has been held by many different tribes over the years, and let's look at a little church situated in Peeblesshire.

We are now getting to my favourite bit, but not just yet...

Stobo Kirk is a church dedicated to St Mungo. Now Saint Mungo and Kentergern are one of the same. Remember the name change thing. It has been said that Kentergern baptised Merlin at birth, and this could have been true. Merlin apparently was covered with hair at birth, and looked a bit like a monster, well his father was a demon, or so it had been believed. But what if his father wasn't a demon, but a Druid and what if his mum was a Christian?

And what if Merlin and Mungo met years later at the battle of 573, though they could have known each other all of their lives (Mungo died in 614) but what if things were not as clear cut as they might seem. We know that the side that Merlin was on was a pagan side, so the battle could be classed as a religious one, Christian verses pagans. This can be found out by going onto the University of Rochester site, and searching up the Camelot Project. It's VERY interesting.

Priests were a common site at any battle, and even the films get that right, so there is no reason to not put these two people together at this point in time.

But what of Merlin going mad isn't as obvious as we think. Berserkers go mad during battle, the Celts were renowned for this; they see red and become unstoppable. Maybe it still isn't clear cut.

Now the next bit is something that I am wondering, and I had not found proof for this or any writings that will back this up, but I will afterwards be looking...as I've only just thought of it

Now according to Legend, Merlin looked after some cool stuff, which was taken to 'The North.'

What if Merlin wasn't mad, as in mad as a hatter, but mad at loosing his friends, his family and the battle, and now, having lost the battle, it now meant that certain things in his possession, or that he was guarding were now under a huge religious threat. Going into a vast forest searching out a hiding place would be a good start, and what if he wasn't just out there in hiding, what if he was finding a safe place to hide something, like, oh lets say the 13 treasures of Britain. One of which belonged to Arthur.

Oh I can almost hear the experts groan.

Well indulge me for a moment. This might not be correct, but it throws up some interesting points.

There are many stories that place Arthur's death before that of Merlin's, so what if that has already happened, was Peredur at Arthurs battles too? Well he was the son of Eliffer, so we know that he was definitely at the 573 one but did Arthur die in that very battle? I don't think so. Oh and incidentally Peredur's death is recorded as happening in 580. The date could be wrong, like so many others, and so we can not rely on dates alone.

48

The battle dates could even be wrong. They are in other chronicles, regarding other battles. But was there only one onslaught, or were there periods of rest within the battle? It is a dubious idea to try and figure out this little, but crucial detail. Could someone have performed a funeral water ritual by breaking a sword and throwing it into a lake, and was then killed, or then continued to fight? Were there other battles taking place in the same district but not the exact same location, at the same time?

What was the terrain like? That also dictates how a battle is delt with. (A quick example is you don't send horsemen into bog land).

The battle has been listed as one of the futile battles, and some annuals put it down to lasting weeks, not just a few hours, but we have been taught, by television, to presume that a battle only takes as long as it's shown in the film. History is not black and white and there is a lot of grey. Look at the siege of Troy, how many years were the Greeks fighting for.

People in the armed forces will know that a skirmish can take but a few minutes, spasmodic, or they can take, well indefinitely. A full on battle, well, we have evidence, especially among the really old Roman, Persian, Greeks texts have stated that they varied considerably. They could last days, nights, and years. There were periods of rest in some of them. Or like Hastings, they took all day, and into the evening. There are no rules to battle; you plan, you adapt and you deal with it; whatever it takes.

What I know is; that we can not take anything for granted.

But where is Arthur in all of this? And why has the nursery rhyme for Old King Cole suddenly popped into my mind? Oh yes, I should have typed Coel Hen, possibly the last Duke of the Roman lot, born 350AD, died around 420AD, and there is a connection to him and all the descendants that were apparently at the battle of 573AD.

The battles that have Arthur in them are in a list below. He may have fought in others, he may have been injured, and unable to fight in the 573 one, who knows. It just takes a bit of common sense and a bit of an imagination to put things into perspective. We are not going to find these mysteries out, as far as I'm concerned the experts are still very much arguing over Marlin, and Arthur and their battles, but here's the list anyway. The Britannia History website has the known details, and is fairly up to date, but you could look up the De Excidio Britanniae by Gildas if you would like an older source.

The battles attributed to Arthur

The 1st battle was at the mouth of the river called Glein

The 2nd, 3rd, 4th, and 5th was at the river Dubglass, in the region of Linnuis; which has a link to what I was saying above.

The 6th battle was on the river called Bassas

The 7th was in the Caledonian forest, this is the battle of Celidon Coit- I thought that that name was actually a person. I also personally think I should tell you at this stage that I don't think for one minute that all of this information is correct, as the dates of some of these battles are way out, but hey ho, on we go!

The 8th was in Guinnion fort

The 9th was in the City of the Legions- a good question to ask at this point is the city one renowned in the past for belonging to the legions or was it the one where the majority of the Romans finally LEFT BRITAIN from, that is an interesting point that NO ONE has ever looked into. Now that could confound a few people!

The 10th was on the banks of the river Tribruit, or possibly Tryfrwyd

The 11th was at the hill called Agned

The 12 was at Badon Hill, as is probably the most famous for most people. Personally I think the eleventh site is interesting. Let's check that out.

The Agned hill has references to the Dolorus Mountains. But it looks like it's going off on a quest of its own, so I'm leaving that train of thought.

Let's leave all the darkness of death behind us now and walk into the golden glow of treasure.

Now I have mentioned that I thought that Merlin might have been hiding the treasures of Britain, or at least that he knew where they were.

I think that my suggestion could be a bit far fetched, as I've just check the list and some of them look like they could be quite big, so he would have needed to transport them in a cart, but let's take a closer look anyway.

I shall give you the list, so you can see what I mean. The 13 treasures list does change over time, so maybe of you want to go down the Celtic road, you can find out why. It's quite interesting.

There was the sword of Rhydderch Hael, do you remember his name? He died in 614, and was Grandad to Constantine of Strathclyde. He was a famous King in the Hen Ogledd text. The year 614 is interesting, a lot of prominent warriors died that year.

The hamper of Gwyddno Garanhir

The horn of Bran Galed

The chariot of Morgan Mwynfawr

The halter of Clydno Eiddyn- Have you noticed that these are all things from heroes?

The knife of Llawfrodedd the horseman

The cauldron of Dyrnwch the giant

The whetstone of Tudwal Tudglyd

The coat of Padarn Beisrudd

51

The crock and dish of Rhygenydd Ysgolhaig

The chessboard of Gwenddoleu ap Ceidio. Arh, and there you have the link to the battles spoken about above, because he died in 573.

The mantle of Arthur in Cornwall, this was basically an invisible cloak, awesome!

The mantle of Tegau Gold-breast

The stone and ring of Eluned the fortunate

Like each of the battle, these were real people, leading real lives and each had their own story to tell, and so do the treasures, for each of them have their story to tell too. So now do you see that I am not completely mad, and the connections are real and important?

Treasure is but one word we can use, how about heirlooms? Were these things handed down to the next generation in royal, tribal or kingship rituals? Surly they were important for the history of this land even if they were now too old to use.

Look to a certain stone of Scotland for an example.

One other thing, the chessboard must have passed into Merlin's possession after that battle of 573, for obvious reasons, and the same could be said for the sword of Rhydderch Hael. Everything that is listed above, are also things that would have been placed into a grave; just something else for you to think about.

Our current Queen was given a load of paraphernalia to hold at her coronation, but it's all of no use to us now is it, so why the ceremony, because it does means something. It is tradition, and that's what I think Merlin was keeping a hold of, and Druids were the keepers of tradition and bloodlines, not to mention all the magical and other stuff associated with them. That thought is mind-blowing when you realise what I am getting at.

But was he the only magical King?

Uther Pen

Taliesin wrote about Uther in 'the death song of Uther Pen.'
It's beautiful, slightly morbid, but most of his poems are.
In the Welsh triads they have another way to describe him.
Uther has been called a shape shifter. So did Merlin have
anything to do with the Igraine incident at all?

In triad 28, he is said to have been the creator of one of the
three enchantments of the Island of Britain, and that he
taught a wizard called Menw. Menw is also a shape shifter
according to the tale of 'Culhwch and Olwen', so did Geoffrey
of Monmouth gets this mixed up also? Is Menw Merlin?

And what are the three enchantments of Britain?

Well, I'm about to disappoint you. You can look at the
triads, but I've read them and they don't really tell you
exactly what the enchantments are, only who received them.
However they are as always, interesting, but why would you
hand down an enchantment? Again, there is no one I can ask.

So let's stick to what we know, or rather what our friend
Geoffrey on Monmouth wrote about him. So consulting his
Historia Britanniae yet again, he puts Uther as the youngest
son of the King of Britain Constantine 11, 407-411 (term of
kingship I believe). His older brother Constans take the
throne but is killed by Vortigern. His brother Aurelius
Ambrosius flees with him to Brittany which has Druid links
from the Boudica revolt times, apparently.

When Vortigern's alliance with the Saxon Hengist breaks
down, Uther returns to Britain and Aurelius kills Vortigern
and becomes king.

But things are still rather turbulent and Uther goes to
Ireland to fight, and also to steal the Giants Ring. While
leading his army back, I presume back home to Britain, and
on his way to meet Vortigern's son in battle, he sees a comet

53

in the sky in the shape of a dragon. The druids that are with him take this as a good sign, and he adopts this golden dragon eventually as his war banner. It becomes his standard. So at least now we know where the dragon part comes from.

Did he ever wear a black helmet with a golden dragon perched on top of it, well how should I know, and yes I'm still trying to find that one on the internet, but I'm having no luck what so ever.

I'm giving up with that now.

If you check out the historical events database, quantrumfuturegroup,org there are some very interesting things going on for around the 19th March, and on till April 400AD. There is a list of citations which include, Socrates Scholasticus who wrote, that in 450 a very large comet stretched from the sky to the ground.

Egh, I just know I'm going to get mixed up with this lot.

In 425 Philostorgius wrote in his Ecclesiasticae Historiae that a sword shape star was in the sky.

The Roman lawyer and historian Hermias Sozomen wrote around 443, that a comet of extraordinary magnitude foretold disaster with regards to the attack on Constantinople.

They have been others too, in 390, 400, the sword shaped one, 442, 451, and 467 was the one that the Byzantium Theophanes wrote about.

Don't take these dates literally, the calendars have been changed again since their times, but modern day experts can trace things like this really easily now. So I'd go down that route if you want to know for sure.

Bede is surprisingly quiet about the whole affair of comets, as far as I can tell. Let me know if I'm wrong. He wrote about one in 729, and that seems to have been it.

So it's fair to say that in the 400's, or there about, were testing times for the skies too. People must have been terrified.

Uther seems to be one of the few people that took the comet as a good sign.

Later he defeats Hengist's son Octa at Verulamium (St Albans), though he is 'wounded' really badly. He is reputed to have been poisoned by the Saxons at a spring. But there is more to this 'wound'.

Ambrosius Aurelianus is also mentioned by Gildas, if you want to cross reference this information.

If you look up earlybritishkingdoms.com you'll get the same type of story; which is now in my own words.

They say that, Uther (410-495) fled to the court of Budic 1. Later after returning to Britain, Uther and Merlin were in Ireland, where Uther acquired the Giants ring- (one of the 13 treasures I wonder, and not a great big stone circle) it also has something to do with the Night of the Long Knives, and I've heard of that before somewhere. Anyway, most of his time was spent fighting the Saxons and the Irish invaders in the North of England. Then he goes off to help the Kings of Strathclyde as they're having problems with the Picts. It is on his return that he encounters Ygerna (Igraine), and that story you already know about.

Later, when he is old and very sick he once again enters into battle (and here we see an echo to the likes of Beowulf)-were these men never allowed to retire, or was a bed-death something they wanted to avoid at all costs? I think they all wanted to die in battle.

So he was fighting the Northern Angles, or rather he was so sick that he had to be carried into St Albans, Verulamium. His army won, but the Angles poisoned the water supply and he died from that.

That is about the best I can give you regarding Uther Pen-Dragon.

But let's see if I can remember what the night of the long knives was, as that's now bugging me.

Arrr, I remember, that it took place somewhere in Wiltshire, it was when Hengist invited all the British chiefs together. They were un-armed, as that was protocol at the time; not to wear your sword at the dinner table, but the Saxon all had concealed weapons and they slaughtered the Britons. That was supposed to have taken place in the year, let me think, 472. But don't quote me on that, my internet's not working, yet again, and I'm going by memory and the expert also think..., wait for it.., that the date is wrong.

The only other thing that I can remember is that only a few escaped, one was called Eldol who was the Earl of Gloucester. He had a stick, if my memory serves me correctly. Vortigern was automatically spared, but only because it fitted into what Hengist and Horsa had planned. Pretty much, the rest of the Earls, thanes and who ever else were there perished. They had been betrayed, and treachery and blood flowed that night as much as the wine had done.

Both Geoffrey of Monmouth and Nennius wrote about it.

That would also explain why Uther hadn't been killed in that horrific betrayal, he probably wasn't there.

Right, let's change the subject and look closer at the giants ring.

The treasure ring has been described; that the wearer of the ring becomes invisible, but although that would be really cool lets look elsewhere.

Well, the Giants ring only comes up with the Neolithic information. My studies took me to a battle of 655, the battle of Farset, but that has nothing to do with what we are talking about. I then looked into the locations of the rivers of Lagan

56

and Farset, but that too was a dead end. The accounts are still interested only in telling us that Uther and Merlin stole the circle of stone, the giants ring and took it across to England. Well, we know that's just not possible, but there is a strong connection between a ring of stone from Ireland and Merlin. But isn't that just a connection to the ring of stones on Salisbury plain, which are in Wiltshire, which is where, according to Nennius, is where the night of the long knives took place.

Ooooo, so now things get very interesting.

I really feel like I'm missing something obvious here, but as yet the answer to that mystery still eludes me. The Giants ring in Belfast apparently was used as a crossing point for pilgrims, but that was in the medieval period, but I can make no further connection to Uther with it.

The ring of stones is still bugging me.

So let's speculate.

The ring from the thirteen treasures made the wearer invisible; maybe the truth was that Uther was in Ireland fighting, he then came back to Britain but Uther's men were not spotted when they hid, or somehow were invisible while his fellows were getting slaughtered on the night of the long knives, which I think was on May Day and at Stonehenge, which was being used as a meeting place. There were reputedly three hundred men on the Briton side alone (who were killed) that would take a big hall to accommodate all that lot, and how many Saxons were there, just as many by the sound of it. Archaeologists can tell you how big the Lords Hall's were in Anglo-Saxon times, but were they big enough to accommodate at least 600 men, their squires, their horses and what ever else was needed at these meetings. Would it not be more logical to have a meeting between to hostile parties out in the open, on a scared site, where arms were not allowed, (that's weapons and not anatomy) where things could be seen, and where both lots had an escape route?

Maybe the Giants Ring was used as the meeting point, but I fear I shall not find that out until after this book has gone to print, and when the experts have had a chance to look into my claim.

I will tell you one thing though, every time I visit Stonehenge, the place feels cold, and even as a child I have always thought of it as hollow place. Maybe there is more to it then the archaeologist have yet found.

I've checked and re-checked and I can find nothing else of note about the night of the long knives, and nothing to do with the fact that it could have been the meeting place. If however someone else has thought of this before, and can prove that they thought of it before me, then I apologise profusely.

But maybe could be onto something there!

Maybe this is the one thing that no one else has considered.

If you go onto the internet and look up kingarthursknights.com, they say that Merlin had been asked by Uther to construct a memorial for his brother Ambrosius and the other lords that had been killed on the night of the long knives. So Merlin headed off to find the Giants Ring, which had healing powers, he finds the ring and it is now what we know as Stonehenge. That's the official story. Why didn't the survivors just get a clerk to write an account down?

Let us now turn our attention back, and let us concentrate on the rituals of the dead.

Burials in the Dark Ages

I am now going to concentrate on three religions, the first of which I can probably rule our almost instantly, but lets take a quick look just to make sure.

Christianity, Celtic and Anglo-Saxon burials

During the Dark Ages, most people still followed their ancestors' way of doing things. However they were varied to say the least. Although later, the church taught that it would be better to be buried as the body was expected to 'raise again,' that doesn't mean that people didn't stop doing what their ancestors had done for generations. There is also the Celtic-Christian church to consider.
The followers of Pelagius, the theologian, loved Christ but never followed the Roman Catholic ways, they were followers of nature, and some would say still fairly Druid-based, although they worshipped Christ, just as they had been doing for generations, and they were sometimes hotly against this newly evolved strain of Christianity, coming out of Rome. So there was still diversity, some people were buried and yet others were cremated, a bit like today. One of the main differences between Christian and pagan burials were the grave goods. Christians, later in time, tended not to be buried with all their worldly goods, they were more likely to just have food and personal items like a comb or a beaded necklace, where as pagans, if they could afford it were buried with masses of stuff, but this was still not strictly true in all cases. It could all have just come down to your personal wealth, or lack of and what you wanted.
 I would love to be able to differentiate between the three, but there does not seem to be much difference.

The clues, if there are any, would be items with symbols on them, such as fish, or the cross, which was by then associated with Christianity, but even then, we are treading on stony ground, especially in a large burial mound, where any items could have come from anywhere.

In short, it would take a remarkable expert to be able to say for sure what religion anyone was, if it was just one body they were looking at.

Archaeologist can delve in a lot deeper, and have the surrounding areas to look at, and any other information, either written in the land, or on a page, will help them out.

Personally, I'm no expert. I'm just using common sense, and going by what the internet says and what I've seen on the archaeological programmes I've watched on TV. I have seen hundreds, and I'm sure we all know what ones I'm referring too, they normally have three day to find out!

So I think I'll be on safer ground if I now concentrate on the four men that are contenders for the Sutton Hoo man.

So without further ado, let's check them out.

The Kings of Sutton Who?

Raedwald

Raedwald was the son of Tytila of East Anglia, and a member of the Wuffingas dynasty, that has connections to King Wuffa, that you may have heard of? He reigned from around 599-624. First he was an under Lord of Aethelberht of Kent. According to Bede, he was the fourth ruler to hold the title imperium. He was the first King of the East Angles to become a Christian, though he still maintained a pagan temple, but then who could blame him? That must have been a shock for the people he ruled over.

Eorpwald

Succeeded his father, Raedwald in about 624, but in 627 or 632 he was murdered by Richberht. There is not much detail about his life, though he could have been killed due to religious differences, as apparently he was the first English king to be killed because he was a Christian.

Sigeberht

Like Eorpwald, he too was considered a Saint. He was probably the younger son of Raedwald, but again not much is known. He was exiled at some point to Gaul. Sigeberht played an important role in making his kingdom Christian, and was praised by Bede for doing so. He abdicated his power to Ecgric, and retired to a monastery at

Beodricesworth, but not to live in peace it seems, a later he was asked to participate in a battle, which he refused.

Ecgric

Bede mentions him in his works. It seems he helped rule East Anglia with his priestly brother Sigeberht. He was killed in battle in around 636 at an unknown location, against Penda. He was probably a pagan. Unlike his brother Sigeberht who refused to fight.

There is little information about these men.
We have to remember that most genealogies and most written evidence were held in monasteries, which of course were attacked by the Vikings during these dark ages, and there is scant evidence left. It is only by piecing together all of the information we have can we even begin to gleam any sort of information.
  And we have to remember, these were real men. They joked, laughed, sang, talked, farted, burped, argued, loved, screamed, cried, and got drunk. They are not just names. Looking at the pitiful amount of knowledge we have about them I'm rather saddened, because we should know more about these men that were buried back in the dark ages, but now lost to time. But are they?
  I shall once again return to the Anglo-Saxon chronicles, as I can not believe that there will be no answers there.
  So I've just trailed through the text once again, and still there seems to be no mention of any of the contenders for Sutton Hoo within those pages. Am I missing something here? I noted Hengist and Horsa in the year 455, but that was the best that I could come up with. I feel rather lame.

Ouroboros

We have come full circle, like an Ouroboros, which is a dragon or snake eating its own tail. It is a devouring beast that like the fiery phoenix rising out of smouldering ashes and flames re-creates itself and can never be extinguished. This is a bit like the tales of both Arthur and Beowulf, for they shall never die.

Up until now it seems it seems like I have been chasing my own tail, or the elusive grail along very dark claustrophobic alleyways, and now I think it is time to ask the King the correct questions, or rather to kneel down on one leg, like a weary knight and present to him my findings.

I could have done this right at the beginning of this book, because I already knew what my heart told me, but did I not ask you reader to use both your heart and your mind while reading this book? So I must do the same. And everyone knows that every story must have a beginning, middle, and an end, and why start off with the answers if you do not know the questions? That was what Percival never realised, he had the answers, but he failed to ask the question.

All stories need false leads, twists and turns and my single question has certainly provided me with them in abundance.

Shall I elaborate?

I believe that the Sutton Hoo man was a fearsome warrior who has stories attached to him, some which are true, and others that are not, and in my mind there is no better candidate than him to be Arthur; the pagan warrior that became Christian. And this may be fanciful, but why not, we need Arthur, we have always needed him.

The human race needs heroes, and we need magic in our lives. We also need to know that there is someone there protecting us, someone that has and will always vanquish our demons and monsters. It is the oldest story of all time, and one like the Ouroboros, one which will never fade or die. So I say, lets keep searching for the lost grail, and one day we might very well find it. Let's keep fighting to ask the correct questions, but let us seek answers both in fact and in fiction, for the two are often laced together. It's only when you walk through the mist that you can then see what lies hidden within.

There is one final and slightly important thing I probably should have added previously. The Sutton Hoo men were buried in East Anglia. Arthur was possibly Cornish, or Welsh or a Scot-if that's the correct term, if it's not, I'm really sorry for the mistake. So, officially, Sutton Hoo man, Arthur and Beowulf are obviously not the actual same person. Beowulf was Scandinavian, and buried in Sweden, at least that's where I think Geatland is.

Putting that tiny detail aside, I shout

Long Live The King!

My conclusion

So is Sutton Hoo, also Beowulf, yes he is, in a way, the same
way that he is Arthur.

If we take even the swiftest look at the artefacts, then we are
instantly taken into the world of Beowulf. He too would have
been adorned with the sword that we see, all garnet and
gold, he too would have stood in a shield wall with the shield
like the one found in the graves of the Sutton Hoo man, he
too would have drank, and spilt his wine or mead from horns,
and would have feasted using plates of silver and gold and he
too would have recognised everything that was buried in the
site of Sutton Hoo. There are so many similarities, just
looking at the artefacts alone, that connect the three men; it
would be ridiculous to say that there were not alike.

All of the three would have heard the same tales, they
would have laughed at the same kind of jokes, and they
would have had their favourite stories, probably one's to do
with hero's and they would have held the same armour, the
same chain mail, and the same helmets. All of them are men
who would have hunted through the forests of Britain,
chasing after boar and stag.

Their lives are lives that had been lived to the full.

They are the heroes of old, the one that fought our dragons,
and they deserve to live in our hearts and minds as such, for
they are the heroes of old.

Resources I referred to for this book

The Roman catafrac
The sarmation cavalry
The Battle of Arfderydd
The Welsh Triads
The Gododdin
The Black Book of Carmarthen
The White Book of Rhydderch
The Red Book of Hergest
The Book of Taliesin
The Nowell Codex
The Narts Saga
Beowulf
The Anglo Saxon Chronicles
The British Chronicles
The Vindolander Letters
The Mabinogion- which also has the Lady of the Fountain in it
The British Museum
The National Trust
The Sutton Hoo Society
The University of Rochester-the Camelot Project
The Hen Ogledd Text
The Battle of Llongborth

People

The Venerable Bede
Geoffrey of Monmouth
Pelagius
Kentergern and St Mungo
Raedwald
Eorpwald
Sigeberht
Ecgric
King Urien
Thomas Malory- Le Morte D'Arthur
Gildas

Www

earlybritishkingdoms.com
quantrumfuturegroup.org
kingarthursknights.com
marres.education/samatic_traces.htm
sacred_text.com
fectio.org.uk.articles/draco.htm
The Britannia History
Glastonburytor.org.uk

Printed in Great Britain
by Amazon

57251751R00041